The Neural Nexus: Physical AI Meets Digital Twin Technology

By Farhana Sethi

"The Neural Nexus: Physical AI Meets Digital Twin Technology" suggests a deep connection or intersection between advanced artificial intelligence (AI) that operates in the physical realm ("Physical AI") and the concept of a "Digital Twin." A digital twin is a virtual replica of a physical object, system, or process, designed to simulate, predict, and optimize real-world performance.

The term "Neural Nexus" hints at the integration of neural-inspired AI—systems that mimic the learning and decision-making processes of the human brain—and digital twin technology. Essentially, this title implies that Physical AI (like AI-powered robots or devices) could have a dynamic, real-time connection to its digital counterpart. This connection would enable enhanced communication, learning, and adaptability, making systems more intelligent and efficient.

It paints a picture of a future where the physical and digital worlds are seamlessly interwoven, creating smarter systems that can anticipate, learn, and react to the ever-changing real-world environment.

Contents

Dedication

To my family, whose unwavering support has been the cornerstone of my journey

About me

I am a multifaceted professional—business leader, technical researcher, writer, developer, and digital content curator—with 20 years of experience in the technology sector. As a Computer Engineer and Technology Leader, I am driven by the endless possibilities of technology, astrophysics, and human psychology. My passion for exploration has taken me to six continents and over 40 countries, and I've had the privilege of living and working on three continents. These experiences have enriched my perspective, deepened my understanding of diverse cultures, and fueled my passion for innovation.

My mission is to bridge technology and humanity, leveraging my expertise to foster meaningful progress, collaboration, and innovation in a world that continues to evolve. Through my work, I strive to inspire others, embrace diverse perspectives, and create solutions that not only advance technology but also improve the lives of people around the globe.

My profile is https://www.fsethi.com

Why I Wrote This Book

In an era defined by the rapid convergence of the physical and digital worlds, it has become increasingly imperative to explore the transformative potential of cutting-edge technologies. This is the genesis of my fascination with what I call "The Neural Nexus"—the intersection of Physical AI and Digital Twin technology. Together, these fields represent not just a technological advancement but a paradigm shift in how we perceive, interact with, and enhance our reality.

Physical AI, at its core, embodies artificial intelligence that exists and operates within the tangible, material world. Whether in the form of autonomous robots or adaptive smart systems, Physical AI is an intelligence that breathes life into machines, granting them the capability to learn, react, and evolve in real time. Meanwhile, Digital Twin technology serves as the virtual counterpart, a meticulously constructed digital replica of physical entities, processes, or systems. This symbiotic relationship between the physical and digital realms fosters a dynamic feedback loop, enabling us to predict, optimize, and innovate with unprecedented precision.

My motivation for this book stems from a desire to not only demystify these emerging technologies but to illuminate their potential to reshape industries, redefine creativity, and address some of humanity's most pressing challenges. From revolutionizing healthcare with hyper-personalized treatments to building sustainable cities through real-time simulation, the possibilities at this neural nexus are as vast as they are exciting.

As we venture further into this exploration, I invite you, dear reader, to consider not just the technical marvels of these innovations but also the profound societal and ethical implications they carry. What does it mean to create a machine that learns as we do? How do we ensure the responsible and equitable use of these technologies in a way that serves humanity? These are the questions that I hope to explore together, one chapter at a time.

Who should read this book

This book is written for a diverse audience, bridging the gap between technical professionals and curious enthusiasts. Here are the groups of people who would find value in reading *The Neural Nexus: Physical AI Meets Digital Twin Technology*:

1. **Tech Innovators and Engineers:** Those at the forefront of AI, robotics, and digital twin technologies will find inspiration and insights into the possibilities and challenges of merging these fields.

2. **Business Leaders and Decision-Makers:** Executives and entrepreneurs interested in leveraging these technologies to drive efficiency, innovation, and competitive advantage in industries like healthcare, manufacturing, energy, and urban planning.

3. **Academics and Researchers:** Students, scholars, and professionals exploring new developments in AI, machine learning, and system modeling would benefit from the depth and breadth of concepts discussed.

4. **Ethicists and Policy Makers:** Those working to shape the ethical and societal frameworks around emerging technologies will find food for thought on critical issues like privacy, equity, and accountability.

5. **Curious Minds:** Tech enthusiasts and futurists intrigued by the possibilities of blending physical and digital realms will enjoy an engaging and accessible journey into these groundbreaking ideas.

6. **Educators:** Teachers and lecturers seeking a resource to introduce or deepen understanding of this cutting-edge topic in their courses.

This book is for anyone eager to explore the intersection of innovation, practicality, and the ethical dimensions of a rapidly changing technological landscape. Who do you envision as your primary readers? Perhaps we can adjust the tone or focus accordingly!

Prologue

We stand at the edge of a remarkable era. The lines between the physical and digital worlds blur more each day, drawing us into an age where technology does more than assist—it collaborates, learns, and evolves alongside us. As I write these words, humanity's ingenuity is transforming how we understand and interact with reality itself. Within this profound shift lies an intersection I call "The Neural Nexus," a convergence of two groundbreaking technologies: Physical AI and Digital Twin technology.

Imagine a world where intelligent machines walk among us—not as distant concepts, but as integrated partners in our daily lives. Picture robots that can anticipate your needs or adapt to their surroundings, enhancing industries, societies, and individual lives. These machines, powered by Physical AI, have the capacity to learn, evolve, and adapt in ways that mimic human intelligence, bringing a new kind of life to the objects around us.

Now, imagine these physical entities mirrored by their digital counterparts: Digital Twins. These are not mere simulations but living, breathing reflections of their real-world counterparts, continuously updated in real time. Digital Twins enable us to experiment, predict outcomes, and optimize complex systems without ever endangering the physical world. It is here, at the intersection of these two realms, that the possibilities become boundless.

This book is a journey into this nexus, a place where innovation flourishes and humanity's potential expands. As an engineer, a technologist, and a dreamer, I have always been captivated by the promise of progress. Yet, with progress comes responsibility. The same tools that can revolutionize healthcare, transform manufacturing, and create sustainable cities also carry profound ethical questions. How do we balance innovation with equity? How do we ensure that these technologies serve all of humanity, not just a privileged few?

The Neural Nexus represents more than a technological shift—it is a call to action. We are the architects of this future, entrusted with the challenge of shaping it responsibly. This book is my attempt to demystify these technologies, to explore their potential, and to ignite conversations that will guide us toward a brighter tomorrow.

As we embark on this exploration together, I invite you to not only marvel at what is possible but to reflect on what is necessary. Technology alone is not the answer; it is a tool that must be wielded with wisdom and care. Let this journey into the Neural Nexus be a catalyst for your imagination, your curiosity, and your sense of purpose. Together, we will chart a course through this fascinating convergence of the physical and digital worlds—and, perhaps, uncover what it truly means to innovate responsibly in an ever-changing world.

Introduction

The technological frontier is constantly shifting, reshaping the way we understand and interact with the world around us. In recent decades, we have witnessed seismic advances in artificial intelligence, robotics, and data sciences, each paving the way for innovations that were once relegated to the realm of science fiction. Among these breakthroughs, two transformative concepts—Physical AI and Digital Twin technology—stand out as catalysts for a new age of intelligence and connectivity.

But what exactly are these concepts, and why do they matter? Physical AI refers to the embodiment of artificial intelligence in the physical world. Unlike traditional AI, which exists primarily in software or virtual environments, Physical AI is tangible—it is intelligence manifested in machines, robots, and systems that can interact with and adapt to the complexities of the real world. These intelligent systems are not static; they learn, evolve, and collaborate, bringing us closer to the vision of machines as autonomous partners rather than mere tools.

Digital Twins, on the other hand, operate in the digital domain, but their connection to the physical world is no less profound. A Digital Twin is a virtual replica of a physical entity, whether that entity is a machine, a building, or an entire city. These twins are more than passive representations; they are dynamic systems that mirror their real-world counterparts in real time, integrating data streams to simulate, analyze, and predict outcomes with astonishing accuracy. By linking the physical and digital realms, Digital Twins enable us to test scenarios, optimize processes, and drive efficiencies that were previously unattainable.

The convergence of these two technologies forms what I call the Neural Nexus. At this nexus, Physical AI and Digital Twins interact and enhance each other, creating systems that are not only intelligent but also deeply interconnected. Imagine a robot—a piece of Physical AI—that operates with the guidance and insights of its Digital Twin. This symbiotic relationship allows the robot to anticipate challenges, adapt to unforeseen circumstances, and continuously refine its performance. Now imagine this principle scaled up across industries, from healthcare to manufacturing, from transportation to urban planning. The possibilities are as vast as they are transformative.

This book is an exploration of those possibilities. It is an attempt to chart the potential and the pitfalls of this Neural Nexus, to examine how these technologies can reshape our world and what responsibilities we must bear as their architects. Through case studies, conceptual frameworks, and forward-looking analyses, I hope to provide not only a roadmap for understanding these technologies but also a vision for their future.

The Neural Nexus is more than a technological milestone—it is a reflection of humanity's ingenuity and its enduring quest for progress. As we venture into this new frontier, we must ask ourselves not only what is possible but what is right. How do we ensure that these technologies are used ethically and equitably? How do we balance innovation with inclusion? And how do we navigate the delicate interplay between human intelligence and artificial intelligence without losing sight of what makes us uniquely human?

These are the questions that this book seeks to address. The journey ahead is as exciting as it is complex, and I invite you to join me as we delve into the fascinating world of Physical AI and Digital Twin technology. Together, let us explore the Neural Nexus and its potential to shape a brighter, smarter, and more connected future.

Chapter 1: The Convergence of Intelligence and Reality

In the sweeping narrative of technological evolution, humanity's quest for understanding and mastery over its surroundings has been marked by key transformative leaps. From the wheel to the internet, each innovation has ushered in profound changes in how we live, work, and interact. We now stand on the precipice of yet another transformative leap: the seamless integration of Physical AI and Digital Twin technology. This fusion represents not just a technological revolution but a fundamental reimagining of reality itself.

The physical and digital realms, long regarded as separate and distinct, are now beginning to merge in unprecedented ways. Physical AI, with its ability to imbue machines with learning and adaptive capabilities, allows for intelligent, autonomous systems to engage directly with the world. Meanwhile, Digital Twin technology provides a dynamic, virtual mirror of physical systems, enabling real-time analysis, simulation, and optimization. Together, they form the Neural Nexus—a convergence where intelligence transcends traditional boundaries and creates a new paradigm for human-machine collaboration.

The Foundations of Physical AI

To grasp the significance of this convergence, one must first understand the individual components. Physical AI is, at its heart, artificial intelligence brought to life in the material world. Unlike its virtual counterparts, which exist solely in software, Physical AI operates within tangible systems—robots, drones, autonomous vehicles, and even adaptive manufacturing systems.

What sets Physical AI apart is its ability to perceive, learn, and adapt in real-time. This intelligence is not static; it evolves through continuous interaction with its environment. For example, consider an autonomous delivery robot navigating a busy urban landscape. Equipped with sensors and machine learning algorithms, it must interpret complex visual and auditory data, predict human behavior, and make split-second decisions to ensure safe and efficient delivery. This level of autonomy and adaptability defines Physical AI and underscores its transformative potential.

Physical AI is deeply rooted in advances in machine learning, computer vision, and robotics. Neural networks, inspired by the structure of the human brain, enable machines to process and interpret vast amounts of data. Reinforcement learning allows systems to improve their performance through trial and error, much like how humans learn new skills. These innovations, coupled with advances in hardware such as sensors and processors, have paved the way for intelligent systems that can thrive in complex, unstructured environments.

The Emergence of Digital Twins

Parallel to the rise of Physical AI is the emergence of Digital Twin technology. A Digital Twin is a virtual representation of a physical object, process, or system, continuously updated with real-time data from its physical counterpart. This dynamic connection allows for a level of insight and control that was previously unimaginable.

The concept of the Digital Twin was first introduced in the context of aerospace engineering, where the ability to simulate and monitor complex systems such as aircraft engines was critical. Today, Digital Twin technology has expanded far beyond aerospace, finding applications in manufacturing, healthcare, urban planning, and beyond.

What makes Digital Twins so powerful is their ability to bridge the gap between the physical and digital worlds. By creating a living, breathing model of a physical system, a Digital Twin allows engineers and operators to monitor performance, predict failures, and optimize processes with unparalleled precision. For example, a Digital Twin of a smart city can integrate data from sensors, weather forecasts, and traffic patterns to optimize energy usage, reduce congestion, and improve quality of life for its residents.

Digital Twins are powered by advancements in data analytics, the Internet of Things (IoT), and cloud computing. By harnessing the vast amounts of data generated by connected devices, Digital Twins provide a holistic view of complex systems, enabling smarter decision-making and more efficient operations.

The Neural Nexus: Where Physical AI Meets Digital Twins

The true potential of these technologies emerges at their intersection—the Neural Nexus. This is where Physical AI and Digital Twin technology combine to create systems that are not only intelligent but also deeply interconnected. At this nexus, the physical and digital worlds merge into a unified whole, enabling unprecedented levels of insight, control, and innovation.

Consider the example of an autonomous factory, where robots powered by Physical AI are guided by Digital Twins of the production line. The Digital Twins continuously analyze data from sensors embedded in the factory, providing real-time insights into efficiency, quality, and maintenance needs. This information is fed back to the robots, allowing them to adapt their actions and optimize the production process. The result is a seamless integration of intelligence and reality, where machines and humans work together to achieve outcomes that were previously unattainable.

The Neural Nexus also has profound implications for industries such as healthcare. Imagine a robotic surgical system powered by Physical AI, guided by the Digital Twin of a patient. The Digital Twin integrates data from medical imaging, patient history, and real-time sensor inputs, creating a comprehensive model of the patient's anatomy and physiology. This model guides the robotic system, ensuring precision, safety, and personalized care. The Neural Nexus enables a level of accuracy and adaptability that transforms the field of medicine, making procedures less invasive and outcomes more predictable.

Challenges and Opportunities

While the Neural Nexus holds immense promise, it also presents significant challenges. The integration of Physical AI and Digital Twin technology requires a level of coordination and interoperability that is not easy to achieve. Standards and protocols must be established to ensure seamless communication between systems. Data privacy and security must be prioritized to protect sensitive information from misuse.

Ethical considerations also come to the forefront. As machines become more intelligent and autonomous, questions arise about accountability, transparency, and the impact on human jobs and livelihoods. How do we ensure that these technologies are used responsibly and equitably? How do we prevent biases in AI systems from perpetuating inequalities? These are critical questions that must be addressed as we navigate this new frontier.

At the same time, the opportunities are immense. The Neural Nexus has the potential to revolutionize industries, enhance sustainability, and improve quality of life on a global scale. By enabling smarter systems and more efficient processes, it can help us address some of humanity's most pressing challenges, from climate change to healthcare access.

Real-World Applications of the Neural Nexus

The convergence of Physical AI and Digital Twin technology is not just a theoretical concept—it is being applied in the real world to solve complex problems and drive innovation. Across industries, organizations are leveraging the Neural Nexus to achieve efficiencies, enhance precision, and open new frontiers of possibility.

Healthcare: A Revolution in Precision Medicine

Healthcare is one of the most promising arenas for the Neural Nexus. Imagine a world where patient care is tailored not just to broad diagnostic categories but to the unique physiology and medical history of each individual. This is the promise of combining Physical AI and Digital Twins in medicine.

Consider robotic surgical systems powered by Physical AI. These systems can perform complex procedures with unparalleled precision, guided by the insights provided by a patient's Digital Twin. The Digital Twin integrates data from sources such as MRI scans, X-rays, and genetic profiles, creating a dynamic and detailed model of the patient's anatomy and health. This allows surgeons to simulate procedures in advance, identify potential risks, and customize their approach to maximize outcomes.

Beyond surgery, Digital Twins of patients can enable continuous monitoring and proactive intervention. For example, a diabetic patient's Digital Twin could integrate real-time data from wearable devices, predicting blood sugar fluctuations and suggesting adjustments to diet or medication. Paired with Physical AI devices, such as insulin pumps capable of learning and adapting to the user's needs, this creates a personalized and responsive approach to healthcare.

The implications are profound: fewer complications, shorter recovery times, and a shift from reactive to preventive medicine. Yet, this also raises important questions about data security and patient privacy, which must be addressed as these technologies become more widespread.

Manufacturing: Intelligent and Adaptive Production

In manufacturing, the Neural Nexus is driving the shift toward Industry 4.0—a new era of smart, interconnected production systems. Factories powered by Physical AI and Digital Twins are no longer static and rigid; they are intelligent, adaptive, and capable of responding to real-time changes in demand and supply.

Imagine an automotive production line where robots equipped with Physical AI assemble vehicles. Each robot is guided by a Digital Twin of the production line, which continuously analyzes data from sensors embedded in machinery and tools. The Digital Twin monitors performance, identifies bottlenecks, and predicts maintenance needs, ensuring seamless operations. Physical AI enables the robots to adapt their movements and processes based on these insights, optimizing efficiency and reducing waste.

This integration extends beyond the factory floor. Digital Twins of supply chains can predict disruptions, optimize logistics, and ensure just-in-time delivery of materials. Combined with autonomous vehicles and drones powered by Physical AI, the entire supply chain becomes a cohesive and intelligent system.

The result is a revolution in manufacturing: faster production cycles, higher quality products, and significant cost savings. However, as with healthcare, the adoption of these technologies requires careful consideration of workforce implications and the need for upskilling.

Smart Cities: Building Sustainable and Connected Communities

Urbanization presents one of the greatest challenges of our time, and the Neural Nexus offers powerful tools for creating smarter, more sustainable cities. By integrating Physical AI with Digital Twins of urban systems, cities can optimize resources, reduce waste, and improve quality of life for their residents.

Take transportation as an example. Digital Twins of traffic networks can integrate data from IoT sensors, GPS systems, and weather forecasts to predict congestion and suggest optimal routes. Autonomous vehicles powered by Physical AI can use these insights to navigate efficiently, reducing emissions and travel times. Public transportation systems can dynamically adjust schedules and capacities based on real-time demand, minimizing delays and overcrowding.

Energy management is another critical application. Digital Twins of buildings can monitor energy usage, predict maintenance needs, and suggest improvements to enhance efficiency. Paired with Physical AI systems, such as adaptive HVAC systems and smart lighting, cities can significantly reduce their carbon footprint.

These technologies also enable more effective disaster management. Digital Twins of cities can simulate scenarios such as floods or earthquakes, guiding emergency response efforts and minimizing risks. Physical AI-powered drones and robots can assist in search-and-rescue operations, delivering supplies and providing critical support in disaster-stricken areas.

The vision of smart cities is both inspiring and complex. While the Neural Nexus offers immense potential, it also requires careful planning, investment, and collaboration across sectors to ensure equitable access and avoid exacerbating existing inequalities.

Ethical and Societal Implications

As we embrace the Neural Nexus, we must confront the ethical and societal implications of these technologies. The integration of Physical AI and Digital Twins raises questions about privacy, equity, and accountability that cannot be ignored.

Privacy and Data Security

At the heart of the Neural Nexus is data—vast amounts of sensitive and personal information generated by devices, systems, and individuals. Ensuring the security and privacy of this data is paramount. Without robust safeguards, there is a risk of misuse, breaches, and loss of trust.

Governments, organizations, and technologists must work together to establish transparent data governance frameworks. These frameworks should prioritize individual consent, data minimization, and secure storage, ensuring that data is used responsibly and ethically.

Equity and Inclusion

The benefits of the Neural Nexus should not be limited to a privileged few. As these technologies are deployed, it is essential to address issues of access and affordability, ensuring that their advantages are distributed equitably across societies.

Efforts must be made to prevent bias in AI systems and to ensure that marginalized communities are not excluded from the opportunities created by the Neural Nexus. This requires proactive policies, inclusive design principles, and a commitment to diversity in the development of these technologies.

Accountability and Ethics

As machines become more intelligent and autonomous, the question of accountability becomes increasingly complex. Who is responsible when an AI system makes a mistake or causes harm? How do we ensure transparency in decision-making processes? These are critical issues that must be addressed through thoughtful regulation and ethical frameworks.

At the same time, we must consider the broader implications of the Neural Nexus on the human experience. How do these technologies impact our relationships, our work, and our sense of identity? As we delegate more responsibilities to intelligent machines, we must ensure that technology enhances, rather than diminishes, what makes us uniquely human.

Conclusion

The emergence of the Neural Nexus—the powerful intersection of Physical AI and Digital Twin technology—represents a pivotal moment in the evolution of intelligence and connectivity. By seamlessly integrating the physical and digital realms, these technologies have the potential to redefine industries, transform cities, and enhance the human experience in ways once thought impossible. From personalized healthcare and adaptive manufacturing to sustainable urban design, the opportunities are vast and transformative.

However, as we delve deeper into this convergence, it becomes clear that technological progress alone is not enough. The challenges of data security, ethical accountability, and equitable access demand our attention and action. The Neural Nexus is not just a technological revolution; it is a societal responsibility—a reminder that innovation must always be guided by wisdom, inclusivity, and humanity.

As we journey further into this book, we will explore the practical applications, philosophical implications, and future possibilities of this remarkable convergence. Together, let us navigate the Neural Nexus, not only as inventors and visionaries but as stewards of a world where technology and humanity coexist harmoniously.

Chapter 2: Origins and Evolution of the Neural Nexus

The story of the Neural Nexus—where Physical AI meets Digital Twin technology—did not emerge overnight. It is a culmination of decades of innovation, incremental advances, and revolutionary breakthroughs in multiple fields. To understand the profound implications of this convergence, we must first trace its origins, exploring the historical milestones and technological catalysts that have shaped its development. This chapter examines the journey of these two fields from their infancy to their fusion into the Neural Nexus.

The Birth of Artificial Intelligence: Pioneering the Concept of Machines That Think

Artificial Intelligence (AI) has long been a subject of human imagination, inspiring countless works of science fiction. However, the roots of AI as a scientific discipline date back to the mid-20th century. In 1956, the Dartmouth Conference brought together brilliant minds to explore the possibility of creating machines capable of mimicking human thought processes. This event marked the formal inception of AI research.

Early AI systems were rule-based, relying on predefined logic and algorithms to perform tasks. These systems, while groundbreaking at the time, lacked adaptability and could not operate effectively in dynamic environments. The limitations of early AI led researchers to explore new approaches, including the development of machine learning algorithms capable of learning from data.

By the 1980s and 1990s, advancements in computing power and the availability of large datasets catalyzed a shift toward data-driven AI. Neural networks, inspired by the structure of the human brain, began to gain traction. These networks laid the groundwork for modern machine learning and deep learning techniques, enabling AI systems to recognize patterns, make predictions, and adapt to new information.

The concept of Physical AI emerged as researchers sought to extend these capabilities beyond software. By integrating AI with robotics and sensing technologies, they began creating machines that could interact with and learn from the physical world. Physical AI represented a new frontier—one that combined the computational power of AI with the tangible presence of robotics.

The Rise of Digital Twins: Virtual Reflections of Reality

While AI was evolving, another field was quietly taking shape: the concept of virtual models that mirrored physical systems. The term "Digital Twin" was first introduced in 2002 by Dr. Michael Grieves during a presentation on product lifecycle management. However, the idea of creating virtual replicas of physical objects dates back even further.

In the aerospace industry, engineers began developing digital models of aircraft and spacecraft to simulate performance and predict failures. These early efforts were driven by the need for safety and efficiency in complex systems. Over time, advancements in computing and data analytics enabled the creation of more sophisticated Digital Twins that could integrate real-time data from sensors embedded in physical systems.

The Internet of Things (IoT) played a pivotal role in the evolution of Digital Twins. By connecting physical devices to the internet, IoT enabled the continuous flow of data between physical systems and their digital counterparts. This dynamic feedback loop allowed Digital Twins to become living, breathing models that reflected the current state of their physical counterparts in real time.

As Digital Twins matured, their applications expanded beyond aerospace to industries such as manufacturing, healthcare, and urban planning. They became indispensable tools for optimizing performance, predicting failures, and simulating scenarios. The rise of cloud computing further accelerated the adoption of Digital Twins, providing the computational power needed to process vast amounts of data.

Technological Catalysts: Paving the Way for the Neural Nexus

The convergence of Physical AI and Digital Twin technology would not have been possible without a series of technological breakthroughs that bridged the gap between the physical and digital realms. These catalysts include advancements in sensors, connectivity, data analytics, and machine learning.

The Fusion of Two Worlds: From Parallel Paths to Convergence

For much of their history, Physical AI and Digital Twin technology evolved along parallel paths, addressing distinct challenges and opportunities. However, their convergence was inevitable. As industries sought smarter, more integrated systems, the potential of combining these technologies became clear.

The Neural Nexus represents the synergy of these two fields—a fusion that amplifies their strengths and addresses their limitations. At this nexus, Digital Twins provide the contextual intelligence needed to guide and inform Physical AI systems. Conversely, Physical AI brings the ability to act and adapt in the real world, closing the loop between simulation and execution.

Consider the example of autonomous vehicles. Digital Twins of road networks can simulate traffic patterns, optimize routes, and predict hazards. Physical AI, embedded within the vehicle, uses this information to navigate safely and efficiently. The interaction between these technologies creates a seamless and intelligent transportation system that adapts to real-time conditions.

The Role of Collaboration: Breaking Silos

The emergence of the Neural Nexus has been driven by collaboration across disciplines, industries, and sectors. Engineers, data scientists, roboticists, and policymakers have come together to address the challenges and harness the opportunities of this convergence.

One of the key lessons from this journey is the importance of breaking down silos. The fusion of Physical AI and Digital Twin technology requires a holistic approach that integrates knowledge from diverse fields. This collaborative spirit has not only accelerated innovation but also fostered a culture of openness and shared learning.

For example, the healthcare industry has seen collaborations between medical professionals, AI researchers, and device manufacturers to create systems that improve patient outcomes. Similarly, smart city initiatives have brought together urban planners, technologists, and local governments to design more sustainable and connected communities.

Looking Ahead: The Road to Transformation

As we reflect on the origins and evolution of the Neural Nexus, it is clear that we are only at the beginning of this transformative journey. The convergence of Physical AI and Digital Twin technology has already begun to reshape industries and redefine possibilities. However, its full potential is yet to be realized.

The road ahead is both exciting and challenging. To unlock the possibilities of the Neural Nexus, we must continue to invest in research, foster collaboration, and address the ethical and societal implications of these technologies. By doing so, we can ensure that the Neural Nexus not only advances technology but also serves humanity.

This chapter has traced the journey of Physical AI and Digital Twin technology from their humble beginnings to their convergence into the Neural Nexus. In the chapters that follow, we will explore the practical applications, societal impact, and future possibilities of this remarkable fusion. Together, we will envision a world where intelligence and connectivity transcend boundaries, shaping a brighter, smarter, and more connected future.

Technological Turning Points: Building the Framework

The path to the Neural Nexus was not linear. It was marked by critical turning points where breakthroughs in one field catalyzed progress in another. One such moment was the advent of the Internet of Things (IoT). By enabling connectivity between devices and physical systems, IoT laid the foundation for Digital Twins to evolve from static models into dynamic, data-driven reflections of reality.

Around the same time, robotics experienced a renaissance, fueled by improved hardware and advanced algorithms. Physical AI systems became increasingly sophisticated, moving beyond programmed actions to adaptive behaviors. In manufacturing, for example, the introduction of collaborative robots—or "cobots"—marked a turning point. These robots, powered by sensors and AI, could work safely alongside humans, learning and adapting in real time.

Simultaneously, advances in simulation software allowed engineers to create Digital Twins with remarkable accuracy. Software platforms capable of integrating real-time data streams became critical tools for industries ranging from aerospace to automotive. This evolution was further bolstered by machine learning algorithms, which brought predictive power to Digital Twins, enabling them to simulate future scenarios with precision.

The convergence of these advancements set the stage for the Neural Nexus. By combining the adaptability of Physical AI with the predictive intelligence of Digital Twins, industries began to glimpse the potential of intelligent, interconnected systems capable of transforming how we interact with the physical world.

The Role of Global Challenges: Accelerating Innovation

While technological progress drove the development of the Neural Nexus, global challenges acted as accelerators. Crises often compel humanity to innovate, and the same has been true for the fields of Physical AI and Digital Twins.

The COVID-19 pandemic, for example, highlighted the importance of remote monitoring and control. Digital Twins became invaluable tools for managing supply chains, optimizing hospital operations, and even modeling virus transmission. Similarly, Physical AI systems, such as autonomous robots, played a critical role in tasks like delivering medical supplies and disinfecting public spaces. The urgency of the pandemic accelerated the adoption of these technologies, demonstrating their value in solving complex, real-world problems.

Climate change has been another driving force. As the world grapples with the need for sustainable practices, the Neural Nexus offers solutions. From optimizing energy consumption in buildings to designing resilient infrastructure, the combination of Physical AI and Digital Twins is enabling more sustainable approaches to resource management.

These global challenges underscore the potential of the Neural Nexus not only as a technological innovation but as a tool for addressing some of humanity's most pressing issues. They also serve as a reminder that the development of these technologies must be guided by a commitment to ethical and equitable practices.

The Neural Nexus in Practice: Case Studies

To illustrate the impact of the Neural Nexus, it is helpful to examine case studies where the integration of Physical AI and Digital Twins has already transformed industries.

Case Study 1: Boeing and Aircraft Maintenance

Boeing, a pioneer in aerospace innovation, has leveraged Digital Twins to enhance aircraft maintenance and performance. By creating Digital Twins of its aircraft, Boeing can monitor wear and tear on components in real time, predict maintenance needs, and prevent costly failures.

The integration of Physical AI further enhances this capability. For example, drones equipped with AI-powered vision systems can inspect aircraft surfaces, identifying cracks or damage with greater accuracy and speed than human inspectors. These drones work in tandem with Digital Twins, ensuring that data collected from inspections is immediately integrated into the virtual model. This allows maintenance teams to take proactive measures, reducing downtime and improving safety.

Case Study 2: Siemens and Smart Manufacturing

Siemens, a global leader in manufacturing technology, has embraced the Neural Nexus in its "Industry 4.0" initiatives. By combining Physical AI with Digital Twins, Siemens has created intelligent factories where production lines are continuously optimized in real time.

In one example, robots on the factory floor are guided by Digital Twins of the manufacturing process. These Digital Twins analyze data from sensors embedded in machines, identifying inefficiencies and suggesting improvements. The robots, equipped with Physical AI, can adapt their actions based on this feedback, ensuring that production runs smoothly and efficiently.

This integration has allowed Siemens to achieve higher productivity, lower costs, and greater flexibility in its manufacturing operations. It also serves as a model for other industries seeking to harness the power of the Neural Nexus.

Case Study 3: Singapore and Smart Cities

Singapore has long been a pioneer in urban innovation, and its efforts to create a smart city exemplify the potential of the Neural Nexus. The city-state has developed Digital Twins of its infrastructure, integrating data from sensors deployed across transportation networks, utilities, and buildings.

These Digital Twins enable city planners to simulate and optimize everything from traffic flow to energy usage. Physical AI systems, such as autonomous buses and adaptive lighting, bring these insights to life, creating a more efficient and sustainable urban environment.

The integration of these technologies has not only improved quality of life for residents but also positioned Singapore as a global leader in smart city development. It demonstrates the potential of the Neural Nexus to address the challenges of urbanization and resource management.

Lessons from the Past: Guiding the Future

The journey to the Neural Nexus offers valuable lessons for the future. Chief among these is the importance of collaboration and cross-disciplinary thinking. The convergence of Physical AI and Digital Twins required the integration of knowledge from fields as diverse as robotics, computer science, engineering, and urban planning. This collaborative approach will be essential as these technologies continue to evolve.

Another lesson is the need for ethical and inclusive practices. The Neural Nexus has the potential to create significant societal benefits, but it also raises questions about privacy, equity, and accountability. As we move forward, it is critical to ensure that these technologies are developed and deployed in ways that serve humanity as a whole, rather than exacerbating existing inequalities.

Finally, the history of the Neural Nexus underscores the power of innovation to address global challenges. From the pandemic to climate change, these technologies have demonstrated their ability to solve complex problems and improve lives. By continuing to invest in research and development, we can unlock their full potential and create a brighter future.

Conclusion

The journey of the Neural Nexus, where Physical AI and Digital Twin technology converge, is a testament to humanity's relentless pursuit of innovation. Tracing its origins, we see how advances in artificial intelligence, robotics, IoT, and data analytics have created a foundation upon which new realities are built. These technologies, once disparate and evolving along parallel paths, have now fused into a transformative force capable of reshaping industries, solving global challenges, and enhancing the human experience.

This chapter has explored the rich history that brought us to this moment: from the nascent beginnings of AI and Digital Twins to the technological breakthroughs and global events that accelerated their development. By examining real-world applications in fields such as aerospace, manufacturing, and urban planning, we have witnessed the immense potential of this convergence to create smarter, more sustainable, and more efficient systems.

Yet, the story of the Neural Nexus is far from over. As we continue to unlock its possibilities, we are reminded that innovation must be guided by responsibility. Ethical considerations, data security, and inclusivity must remain at the forefront to ensure that the benefits of these technologies are shared equitably and responsibly.

Looking ahead, the Neural Nexus stands as both a challenge and an opportunity—a call to collaborate, create, and think beyond the boundaries of what is possible. The chapters that follow will delve deeper into its applications, implications, and the road toward building a world where the physical and digital realms unite harmoniously.

Through understanding its past and envisioning its future, we prepare ourselves to not only navigate this technological frontier but to shape it with wisdom and purpose.

Chapter 3: Applications Across Industries

The Neural Nexus, born out of the convergence of Physical AI and Digital Twin technology, represents a transformative leap forward not only in technology but also in how we solve problems, create efficiencies, and reimagine entire industries. With these capabilities, businesses, governments, and researchers are pioneering new applications that harness the combined power of intelligent physical systems and dynamic digital counterparts. This chapter delves into the myriad ways the Neural Nexus is being applied across industries and highlights the opportunities and challenges that accompany this evolution.

1. Healthcare: Revolutionizing Patient Care

One of the most profound and far-reaching impacts of the Neural Nexus lies in the realm of healthcare. By leveraging Digital Twins and Physical AI, healthcare providers are transforming patient care from a reactive model to one that is predictive, personalized, and preventive.

Personalized Medicine with Patient Digital Twins

Imagine a patient undergoing treatment for a chronic illness such as heart disease. Through advanced imaging, wearable health sensors, and genetic data analysis, a Digital Twin of the patient is created. This Digital Twin becomes a detailed, real-time model of their health, integrating data streams from wearable devices, medical records, and even environmental factors. It tracks the progression of the patient's condition, simulates the effects of different treatment options, and offers physicians tailored recommendations.

For instance, a cardiac surgeon planning a bypass operation can test procedures on the Digital Twin, assessing potential risks and identifying the safest approach. Physical AI systems, such as robotic surgical assistants, execute the procedure with unparalleled precision, guided by the Digital Twin's insights.

Proactive Monitoring and Remote Intervention

For patients with chronic illnesses, the Neural Nexus enables continuous health monitoring. Wearable devices collect data on vital signs, blood sugar levels, or oxygen saturation, feeding updates to the patient's Digital Twin. If abnormalities are detected, the system alerts healthcare providers, enabling swift intervention.

Take the case of diabetes management. A patient's Digital Twin continuously monitors blood glucose levels using data from a wearable glucose sensor. This information is used to predict fluctuations, suggest dietary changes, or adjust medication dosages in real time. Physical AI-powered insulin pumps respond immediately, delivering precise amounts of insulin based on the Digital Twin's analysis.

Such innovations have the potential to improve outcomes, reduce hospitalizations, and empower patients to manage their health more effectively. However, the widespread implementation of the Neural Nexus in healthcare also raises questions about privacy, data ownership, and equitable access to technology.

2. Manufacturing: Building the Factory of the Future

The integration of Physical AI and Digital Twin technology is driving a new era of smart, connected manufacturing systems. Often referred to as "Industry 4.0," these factories leverage the Neural Nexus to optimize processes, minimize waste, and boost productivity.

Intelligent Production Lines

In traditional manufacturing, inefficiencies often go unnoticed until they lead to defects, delays, or costly shutdowns. The Neural Nexus eliminates these blind spots by creating Digital Twins of production lines, machines, and even entire factories. These twins simulate operations in real time, identifying bottlenecks, predicting maintenance needs, and suggesting process improvements.

Physical AI plays a pivotal role in implementing these insights. Robots powered by Physical AI adapt to changes on the production floor, whether it's adjusting to a new product design or reallocating resources in response to a supply chain disruption. These adaptive systems reduce downtime and ensure that production runs smoothly.

For example, automotive manufacturers are using Digital Twins of assembly lines to test the introduction of new vehicle models without disrupting existing operations. Physical AI robots, guided by these simulations, seamlessly switch between tasks, enhancing flexibility and reducing costs.

Predictive Maintenance and Sustainability

Equipment failure is a major challenge in manufacturing, often leading to unplanned downtime and significant financial losses. By using Digital Twins to monitor the health of machines, manufacturers can predict when maintenance is required and avoid costly disruptions. Sensors collect data on vibration, temperature, and performance, feeding it to the Digital Twin, which analyzes patterns and flags potential issues.

Physical AI systems complement this approach by performing maintenance tasks autonomously. Robots equipped with AI can diagnose problems, order replacement parts, and even carry out repairs, ensuring that machines remain operational.

The combination of predictive maintenance and intelligent automation also contributes to sustainability. By reducing waste, optimizing energy usage, and extending the lifespan of equipment, the Neural Nexus enables manufacturers to operate more responsibly and efficiently.

3. Urban Development: Building Smarter Cities

As urbanization accelerates, cities face mounting challenges related to congestion, resource management, and quality of life. The Neural Nexus offers powerful tools for creating smarter, more connected urban environments.

Transportation and Traffic Management

In many cities, traffic congestion is a daily frustration for residents and a significant contributor to carbon emissions. By combining Digital Twins of transportation networks with Physical AI systems, cities can address these challenges more effectively.

Digital Twins simulate traffic patterns, integrating data from GPS systems, cameras, and IoT sensors. They predict congestion, identify optimal routes, and suggest changes to traffic flow. Autonomous vehicles, powered by Physical AI, use these insights to navigate efficiently, reducing delays and emissions.

For example, in Singapore, Digital Twins of the city's road network are used to optimize public transportation schedules and manage ride-sharing services. Physical AI-powered buses and trains dynamically adjust routes and capacities based on real-time demand, improving efficiency and reducing overcrowding.

Energy and Resource Optimization

Smart cities also leverage the Neural Nexus for energy management. Digital Twins of buildings and utilities monitor energy consumption, predict maintenance needs, and identify opportunities for optimization. Adaptive HVAC systems, powered by Physical AI, adjust heating and cooling in response to occupancy patterns and weather forecasts, reducing energy waste.

In addition to buildings, the Neural Nexus plays a role in managing water resources. Digital Twins of water distribution networks monitor pressure, flow rates, and usage, helping cities reduce leaks and improve efficiency. Physical AI-enabled drones assist in inspecting pipelines and performing repairs in hard-to-reach areas.

By integrating these technologies, cities can achieve greater sustainability, resilience, and livability, paving the way for a more connected future.

4. Energy and Utilities: Powering a Sustainable Future

The Neural Nexus is transforming the energy sector by enabling smarter grids, optimizing renewable energy systems, and enhancing reliability in utilities.

Renewable Energy Optimization

As the world transitions to renewable energy, managing the variability of sources like solar and wind becomes a critical challenge. Digital Twins of power grids simulate energy generation, storage, and consumption, ensuring that supply meets demand in real time. Physical AI systems, such as automated wind turbines or solar trackers, adjust their performance based on these simulations, maximizing efficiency.

For instance, a wind farm equipped with Digital Twins and Physical AI can predict changes in wind patterns, adjust turbine angles, and allocate power to storage or distribution systems as needed. This level of intelligence reduces downtime and ensures a consistent energy supply.

Grid Management and Disaster Resilience

Power outages and grid failures can have devastating consequences, particularly during natural disasters. By using Digital Twins to monitor grid performance and predict vulnerabilities, utility companies can proactively address issues before they escalate.

Physical AI systems, such as autonomous inspection drones, assist in identifying damaged infrastructure and performing repairs. During disasters, these systems play a critical role in restoring power quickly and safely, minimizing disruptions for communities.

The integration of the Neural Nexus into energy and utilities not only enhances reliability but also supports the global transition to sustainable energy systems.

5. Aerospace and Defense: Enhancing Safety and Efficiency

The aerospace and defense industries have long been at the forefront of innovation, and the Neural Nexus is no exception. By combining Digital Twins with Physical AI, these sectors are achieving new levels of safety, efficiency, and adaptability.

Aircraft Maintenance and Operations

Digital Twins of aircraft are revolutionizing maintenance by providing real-time insights into performance and wear. By integrating data from sensors on engines, wings, and other components, these twins predict failures and optimize maintenance schedules. Physical AI-powered robots assist in inspections, repairs, and upgrades, ensuring that aircraft remain in peak condition.

Additionally, Digital Twins are used to simulate flight operations, testing different scenarios and improving decision-making. For example, during emergencies, pilots can rely on insights from the Digital Twin to navigate complex situations with confidence.

Autonomous Systems and Defense Applications

In defense, the Neural Nexus is enabling the development of intelligent, autonomous systems. Unmanned aerial vehicles (UAVs), powered by Physical AI, operate in coordination with Digital Twins of the battlefield, providing real-time situational awareness and enhancing mission effectiveness.

These systems are not limited to combat scenarios; they also play a role in disaster relief and humanitarian efforts. For instance, UAVs equipped with Physical AI can deliver supplies to remote areas, guided by Digital Twins of terrain and weather conditions.

The integration of the Neural Nexus into aerospace and defense underscores its potential to improve safety, efficiency, and resilience in critical systems.

Challenges and Opportunities Across Industries

While the applications of the Neural Nexus are vast and varied, its implementation is not without challenges. Data security, interoperability, and scalability are common concerns across industries. Ensuring that these technologies are accessible, ethical, and inclusive requires collaboration between governments, businesses, and technologists.

At the same time, the opportunities are immense. By addressing real-world problems with intelligence and precision, the Neural Nexus has the potential to drive economic growth, enhance sustainability, and improve quality of life on a global scale.

Conclusion

Chapter 3 has explored the practical applications of the Neural Nexus across industries, from healthcare and manufacturing to urban development and aerospace. These examples illustrate the transformative potential of combining Physical AI and Digital Twin technology to create smarter, more efficient, and more sustainable systems. As we continue to unlock the possibilities of this convergence, the challenges of implementation and ethical responsibility remain critical considerations. The chapters that follow will delve deeper into the societal implications, philosophical questions, and future possibilities of this remarkable technological evolution.

Chapter 4: Ethical Considerations and Societal Impacts

Technological revolutions are often hailed for their ability to solve pressing problems, streamline operations, and introduce efficiencies that were previously unimaginable. Yet, with every leap in innovation comes a responsibility to assess not only the opportunities but also the risks and repercussions. The Neural Nexus—a powerful convergence of Physical AI and Digital Twin technology—is no exception. This chapter explores the critical ethical considerations and societal impacts tied to this transformative innovation, discussing issues of privacy, fairness, accountability, and the broader implications for the human experience.

1. The Question of Privacy: Who Controls the Data?

At the core of the Neural Nexus lies an immense reliance on data. The systems enabled by Physical AI and Digital Twins are fueled by a constant stream of real-time information, whether from wearable health devices, industrial sensors, or urban monitoring networks. While this data is indispensable for the functionality of these technologies, it also raises pressing questions about privacy.

The Risk of Over-Surveillance

Consider a smart city where Digital Twins monitor transportation networks, building systems, and energy grids. While these simulations enable efficiency and sustainability, they also depend on collecting data about citizens' movements, behaviors, and preferences. This creates a potential risk of over-surveillance, where the boundaries between public safety and personal privacy become blurred.

The ethical question then arises: Who owns this data, and how can its collection be regulated to prevent misuse? Without adequate safeguards, there is the danger of creating surveillance systems that infringe on individual freedoms and empower those in control with unprecedented oversight over citizens' lives.

Transparency and Consent

One of the most critical aspects of addressing privacy concerns is ensuring that individuals and organizations understand how their data is being used. Transparency must be a foundational principle of the Neural Nexus. Organizations implementing these technologies need to clearly communicate their data collection practices, seeking informed consent from all stakeholders.

For example, in healthcare applications, patients must be made aware of how their personal health data is used to create Digital Twins and guide Physical AI systems. Who has access to this data? How is it stored? How long is it retained? Addressing these questions is essential to building trust and ensuring ethical practices.

2. Equity and Accessibility: Avoiding Technological Disparities

The Neural Nexus has the potential to revolutionize industries and improve quality of life across the globe. However, without careful planning, its benefits could be unevenly distributed, exacerbating existing inequalities rather than alleviating them.

The Digital Divide

One of the primary challenges in ensuring equity is addressing the digital divide—the gap between those who have access to technology and those who do not. The Neural Nexus relies on sophisticated infrastructure, high-speed connectivity, and advanced devices, which may be out of reach for underserved communities or developing nations.

For instance, while a wealthy urban center might implement Digital Twins to optimize transportation and energy use, a rural area with limited internet access could struggle to adopt even the most basic elements of these technologies. Without proactive measures, this divide could lead to a world where the benefits of the Neural Nexus are enjoyed exclusively by affluent regions, leaving others further behind.

Ethical Deployment in Healthcare and Beyond

Equity issues extend to specific industries as well. In healthcare, for example, Digital Twins and Physical AI have the potential to personalize treatments and improve outcomes, but their cost could make them inaccessible to underserved populations. Ethical deployment requires a commitment to creating affordable solutions and ensuring that resources are allocated fairly.

Collaboration between governments, private companies, and non-profits will be essential in addressing these disparities. Subsidies, public-private partnerships, and inclusive design principles can help bridge the gap, ensuring that the Neural Nexus serves as a tool for global progress rather than a driver of inequality.

3. The Future of Work: Transformation or Displacement?

The integration of the Neural Nexus into industries such as manufacturing, transportation, and healthcare is poised to transform the workforce. Physical AI systems, guided by Digital Twins, bring unprecedented efficiency and precision, but they also raise concerns about job displacement and the redefinition of work.

Automation and Job Losses

In industries like manufacturing, where robots powered by Physical AI already perform tasks traditionally handled by humans, the widespread adoption of the Neural Nexus could accelerate automation. Digital Twins simulate and optimize production processes, making it possible for companies to achieve higher outputs with fewer workers. While this creates efficiencies, it also threatens the livelihoods of those employed in repetitive or manual roles.

The ethical question here is not whether automation should occur—it is likely inevitable—but how society can support workers impacted by these changes. Reskilling programs, social safety nets, and policies that promote job creation in emerging fields will be critical to ensuring a just transition.

Redefining Human Roles

At the same time, the Neural Nexus has the potential to create new opportunities and redefine human roles within the workforce. Instead of replacing workers, Physical AI and Digital Twins can augment human capabilities, enabling people to focus on creative, strategic, and high-value tasks.

For example, in healthcare, rather than replacing doctors, Digital Twins can provide insights that enhance decision-making and improve patient outcomes. Similarly, in manufacturing, workers might shift from manual labor to roles that involve overseeing, programming, or collaborating with intelligent systems. This shift emphasizes the need for education and training programs that prepare the workforce for a future where humans and machines work side by side.

4. Accountability and Ethics in Intelligent Systems

As Physical AI systems become more autonomous and Digital Twins play an increasingly central role in decision-making, questions of accountability and ethics come to the forefront. Who is responsible when an intelligent system makes a mistake, and how can we ensure these systems operate in ways that align with human values?

Algorithmic Bias and Fairness

One of the challenges in deploying AI systems is addressing algorithmic bias. Because AI is trained on historical data, it can inadvertently perpetuate biases present in that data. In the context of the Neural Nexus, biased algorithms could lead to unfair outcomes in areas ranging from hiring decisions to healthcare treatments.

For example, a biased AI system guiding a Digital Twin in healthcare might prioritize treatment options that are less effective for certain demographics. Addressing this requires diverse and inclusive datasets, rigorous testing, and ongoing oversight to ensure fairness and accuracy.

Autonomous Systems and Liability

As Physical AI systems gain autonomy, the question of liability becomes increasingly complex. If an autonomous vehicle powered by the Neural Nexus is involved in an accident, who is responsible—the manufacturer, the operator, or the system itself? Similar questions arise in other industries, from healthcare to manufacturing.

Establishing clear regulatory frameworks and ethical guidelines will be essential in addressing these challenges. Transparency in system design, explainability of AI decisions, and mechanisms for accountability must be prioritized to ensure public trust in these technologies.

5. Broader Societal Impacts: Rethinking Human Experience

Beyond specific ethical and operational concerns, the Neural Nexus has broader implications for the human experience. By merging the physical and digital realms, it challenges our understanding of reality, relationships, and identity.

The Nature of Interaction

The integration of intelligent systems into our daily lives alters how we interact with the world around us. Physical AI systems, such as autonomous delivery robots or AI-powered assistants, introduce new forms of interaction that are both convenient and impersonal. While these systems improve efficiency, they also raise questions about the value of human-to-human interaction and the potential for social isolation.

Dependence on Technology

As the Neural Nexus becomes more integrated into critical systems, society's dependence on technology will deepen. While this dependence enables remarkable advances, it also creates vulnerabilities. System failures, cyberattacks, or natural disasters could disrupt essential services powered by the Neural Nexus, highlighting the need for robust safeguards and contingency plans.

The Ethics of Enhancement

Finally, the Neural Nexus raises philosophical questions about the ethics of enhancement. As Digital Twins become more sophisticated and Physical AI systems gain capabilities that surpass human limitations, society must grapple with what it means to enhance ourselves and our environments. How do we balance the benefits of these technologies with the preservation of our humanity? These are questions that require careful consideration and collective reflection.

Conclusion

The Neural Nexus represents a profound technological convergence with the potential to transform industries, solve global challenges, and enhance the human experience. However, its adoption also brings with it a host of ethical considerations and societal impacts that must be addressed thoughtfully and responsibly.

As we navigate this ethical landscape, transparency, inclusivity, and accountability must guide our actions. By proactively addressing privacy concerns, ensuring equitable access, supporting workforce transitions, and establishing clear ethical frameworks, we can harness the full potential of the Neural Nexus while mitigating its risks.

This chapter underscores the importance of viewing technology not just as a tool for progress but as a reflection of our values and priorities. In the chapters that follow, we will explore how these ethical considerations influence the implementation of the Neural Nexus and its role in shaping the future of human-machine collaboration.

Chapter 5: Future Possibilities and the Road Ahead

As the Neural Nexus continues to evolve, it heralds a future filled with possibilities that push the boundaries of technology, innovation, and human imagination. The convergence of Physical AI and Digital Twin technology has already begun reshaping industries and societies, but its full potential lies ahead. In this chapter, we will explore the visionary applications, emerging technological frontiers, and strategic pathways that will define the road ahead for the Neural Nexus.

1. The Visionary Applications of Tomorrow

While the Neural Nexus is already driving transformative change in areas such as healthcare, manufacturing, and urban development, its future applications promise to venture into uncharted territories. These innovations will redefine what is possible, unlocking new levels of intelligence, interconnectivity, and creativity.

Personalized Education Systems

Imagine a future where every student has a Digital Twin that represents their unique learning style, strengths, and weaknesses. This Digital Twin, informed by data from educational assessments, classroom interactions, and even cognitive studies, becomes a personalized learning guide. It suggests tailored curricula, recommends effective study techniques, and identifies areas where additional support is needed.

Physical AI systems, such as adaptive educational robots or immersive virtual reality (VR) platforms, bring these insights to life. These systems adjust their teaching methods in real time based on the feedback from the student's Digital Twin, creating an engaging and customized learning experience. Such innovations could revolutionize education, making it more inclusive and effective for diverse learners across the globe.

Space Exploration and Colonization

As humanity ventures further into space, the Neural Nexus will play a central role in enabling exploration and colonization. Spacecraft equipped with Physical AI systems, guided by Digital Twins of planetary environments, can adapt to the challenges of interplanetary travel and settlement.

For instance, Digital Twins of spacecraft simulate the stresses of deep-space missions, predicting failures and optimizing performance. On planetary surfaces, Digital Twins of habitats integrate data from sensors monitoring temperature, radiation, and oxygen levels, ensuring the safety and comfort of human settlers. Physical AI robots perform maintenance, construct habitats, and assist in scientific research, creating a seamless synergy between technology and human presence in space.

Creative Collaboration and Art

The Neural Nexus also holds the potential to revolutionize creativity, enabling new forms of artistic expression and collaboration. Artists, musicians, and writers could work alongside Physical AI systems that generate ideas, simulate creative processes, and provide real-time feedback.

For example, a composer might collaborate with a Digital Twin of an orchestra, experimenting with different arrangements and receiving instant auditory feedback. Physical AI-powered instruments adapt their tone and style to the composer's preferences, creating a dynamic and interactive creative process. Such innovations not only expand the boundaries of creativity but also democratize access to artistic tools and resources.

2. Emerging Technological Frontiers

To realize these visionary applications, several emerging technological frontiers must be explored and advanced. These areas represent the next steps in the evolution of the Neural Nexus, paving the way for even greater integration and functionality.

Quantum Computing and Advanced Simulations

One of the most exciting frontiers is the integration of quantum computing with the Neural Nexus. Quantum computers, with their ability to process vast amounts of data simultaneously, could revolutionize the capabilities of Digital Twins. Complex simulations that currently require hours or days could be performed in seconds, enabling real-time insights at an unprecedented scale.

For instance, in healthcare, quantum-enhanced Digital Twins could simulate the effects of thousands of drug combinations on a patient's physiology, identifying optimal treatments with unparalleled precision. In energy, quantum simulations could optimize grid performance and renewable energy systems in real time, addressing the challenges of variability and demand.

Brain-Machine Interfaces (BMIs)

The development of brain-machine interfaces represents another frontier with profound implications for the Neural Nexus. BMIs enable direct communication between the human brain and physical or digital systems, creating new possibilities for interaction and control.

Imagine a surgeon using a BMI to guide a Physical AI robotic assistant during a complex operation. The surgeon's thoughts and intentions are translated into precise actions, enhancing dexterity and precision. Similarly, a Digital Twin of the surgeon's brain provides real-time insights into cognitive load and decision-making, optimizing performance and reducing fatigue.

BMIs also hold promise for accessibility, enabling individuals with disabilities to interact seamlessly with Physical AI systems and Digital Twins. By bridging the gap between human cognition and machine intelligence, BMIs bring us closer to a truly integrated Neural Nexus.

Ethical AI and Autonomous Systems

As Physical AI systems become more autonomous, the development of ethical AI becomes increasingly important. Autonomous systems must be designed to operate transparently, make fair decisions, and align with human values.

Emerging research in explainable AI (XAI) aims to address these challenges by creating algorithms that provide clear and understandable explanations for their actions. When combined with the Neural Nexus, XAI ensures that decisions made by Physical AI systems and Digital Twins are accountable and trustworthy.

3. Strategic Pathways to Realizing the Neural Nexus

While the possibilities of the Neural Nexus are vast, realizing its full potential requires strategic planning, investment, and collaboration. Several pathways can guide this journey, ensuring that the technology develops responsibly and sustainably.

Research and Development

Continued investment in research and development is essential to advancing the Neural Nexus. Governments, academic institutions, and private companies must collaborate to address technical challenges, explore new applications, and push the boundaries of what is possible.

Public funding for foundational research in areas such as AI, robotics, and data analytics will play a critical role in driving innovation. At the same time, partnerships between industry leaders and startups can accelerate the development of practical solutions and bring them to market.

Building Infrastructure

The Neural Nexus relies on robust infrastructure to function effectively. High-speed connectivity, edge computing networks, and secure data storage systems are critical components of this infrastructure. Governments and organizations must prioritize the development of these systems to enable widespread adoption of the Neural Nexus.

For instance, the rollout of 5G networks and advancements in cloud computing will provide the low-latency, high-bandwidth connectivity needed to support real-time interactions between Physical AI systems and Digital

Twins. Additionally, investments in cybersecurity infrastructure will ensure that these systems remain secure and resilient against threats.

Establishing Ethical Guidelines

As discussed in Chapter 4, ethical considerations are central to the development and deployment of the Neural Nexus. Establishing clear guidelines and regulatory frameworks will be essential in addressing concerns around privacy, fairness, and accountability.

These guidelines should be developed collaboratively, incorporating input from technologists, ethicists, policymakers, and community stakeholders. They should prioritize transparency, inclusivity, and the equitable distribution of benefits, ensuring that the Neural Nexus serves the common good.

4. The Human Element: Navigating Change

While technology is at the heart of the Neural Nexus, its success ultimately depends on the people who design, implement, and interact with it. Navigating the changes brought about by this convergence requires a focus on the human element.

Education and Workforce Development

As the Neural Nexus transforms industries, education and workforce development must evolve to prepare individuals for the jobs of the future. Schools and training programs should emphasize skills such as critical thinking, creativity, and collaboration, as well as technical expertise in AI, robotics, and data analysis.

Upskilling and reskilling initiatives will be particularly important for workers in industries affected by automation. Governments and businesses must work together to provide accessible training opportunities, enabling individuals to adapt to new roles and thrive in a changing economy.

Public Engagement and Awareness

Building public trust in the Neural Nexus requires transparent communication and meaningful engagement with communities. People must understand how these technologies work, what benefits they offer, and what risks they pose.

Public forums, educational campaigns, and collaborative design processes can help demystify the Neural Nexus and ensure that its development aligns with the values and priorities of society.

5. The Path Forward: A Call to Action

As we look to the future of the Neural Nexus, it is clear that its potential is vast, but its realization will require concerted effort and collective responsibility. The path forward is not without challenges, but it is also filled with opportunities to create a world that is smarter, more connected, and more equitable.

This chapter has outlined visionary applications, emerging frontiers, and strategic pathways that will shape the road ahead. By embracing these opportunities and addressing these challenges, we can unlock the full power of the Neural Nexus and ensure that it serves as a force for good in the world.

As we move forward, let us remember that the Neural Nexus is not just a technological innovation—it is a reflection of humanity's ingenuity, creativity, and values. Its success depends not only on the machines we build but also on the decisions we make and the principles we uphold. Together, we have the opportunity to shape a future where technology and humanity thrive in harmony.

Chapter 6: The Neural Nexus: Physical AI Meets Digital Twin Technology

Digital twin technology and physical artificial intelligence (AI) are converging to form what many call the "neural nexus." This dynamic synergy is reshaping how we interact with and manage physical systems, offering unprecedented opportunities for predictive modeling, optimization, and real-time decision-making. The integration of digital twins with physical AI is particularly transformative in healthcare, manufacturing, and smart cities. By simulating and analyzing real-world systems, these technologies enhance efficiency, sustainability, and innovation. This chapter explores their combined impact and outlines how this neural nexus is revolutionizing industries.

Applications in Healthcare

The healthcare sector has been a frontrunner in leveraging digital twin technology and physical AI, transforming patient care, diagnostics, and treatment processes.

1. Personalized Medicine Digital twins of patients—often referred to as "virtual replicas"—are revolutionizing personalized medicine. By leveraging AI-driven analytics, these twins simulate disease progression, predict treatment outcomes, and optimize therapeutic strategies. For instance:

- *Example*: Companies like Unlearn.AI are developing AI-driven patient twins to improve the efficiency of clinical trials, significantly reducing costs and time.

- *Statistic*: According to MarketsandMarkets, the global digital twin healthcare market is projected to reach $5.1 billion by 2030, growing at a CAGR of 22.2%.

2. Enhanced Surgical Planning Surgeons are increasingly relying on digital twins to plan and rehearse complex surgeries. By creating highly detailed virtual models of organs or entire body systems, these tools allow surgeons to anticipate challenges and refine their techniques. For instance:

- *Example*: In cardiology, digital twins of the heart enable the precise positioning of stents or pacemakers.

- *Emerging Tool*: The MIT-developed HeartFlow Analysis uses AI to model coronary arteries and predict blockages with unparalleled accuracy.

3. Drug Discovery and Development AI-enabled digital twins expedite the drug discovery process by modeling biological systems and simulating interactions at the molecular level. This approach reduces the dependency on animal models and accelerates time-to-market for new drugs. For example:

- *Stat*: A study by Deloitte suggests that AI-integrated digital twins can reduce R&D costs by up to 30%.

4. Remote Patient Monitoring Wearable devices paired with digital twins enable continuous monitoring of patients. AI interprets the data to detect anomalies, predict health issues, and recommend interventions. For example:

- *Example*: IBM Watson is creating comprehensive digital health solutions that integrate wearable data with digital twins to personalize patient care.

Applications in Manufacturing

The manufacturing industry is a prime example of how the neural nexus is driving innovation, cost savings, and operational efficiency.

1. Predictive Maintenance Predictive maintenance has emerged as one of the most impactful applications of digital twin technology. By analyzing real-time data from equipment sensors, AI-powered twins predict machine failures before they occur. This reduces downtime and extends the lifespan of machinery.

- *Example*: Siemens Energy employs digital twins to monitor gas turbines, ensuring seamless operation.

- *Stat*: A report by McKinsey highlights that predictive maintenance can reduce factory downtime by 50% and maintenance costs by 30%.

2. Process Optimization By simulating production processes, digital twins identify inefficiencies and recommend adjustments to optimize resource allocation. AI enhances these simulations by incorporating real-time data and predictive analytics.

- *Example*: Boeing uses digital twins to streamline its aircraft manufacturing processes, achieving higher precision and faster assembly times.

3. Quality Control AI-integrated digital twins enable real-time monitoring and quality assessment in production lines. Defects can be identified and rectified almost instantly, ensuring consistent product quality.

- *Case Study*: A European automotive company reduced defects in its assembly line by 25% after deploying AI-enhanced digital twins.

4. Workforce Training Digital twins serve as interactive training platforms for workers. By simulating manufacturing environments, they provide hands-on learning experiences in a safe virtual setting.

- *Emerging Trend*: The use of virtual reality (VR) in tandem with digital twins for workforce training is expected to grow by 40% annually over the next five years.

Applications in Smart Cities

The concept of smart cities is evolving rapidly, and the neural nexus is central to this transformation. Digital twins integrated with physical AI provide innovative solutions for urban planning, sustainability, and disaster management.

1. Urban Planning and Development Digital twins of cities allow urban planners to simulate infrastructure changes, assess their impact, and make informed decisions. AI enhances these models by incorporating real-time data on traffic, population, and energy consumption.

- *Example*: The city of Singapore has developed a digital twin to manage urban development and simulate new construction projects.

2. Disaster Preparedness and Response Smart cities can leverage digital twins to model natural disasters like floods, earthquakes, or hurricanes. AI-driven analytics provide actionable insights for disaster preparedness and response.

- *Case Study*: In Rotterdam, a digital twin of the city's water management system helps predict and mitigate flood risks.

3. Energy and Sustainability Digital twins are instrumental in optimizing energy consumption and promoting sustainability in urban environments. AI analyzes data from power grids, buildings, and vehicles to enhance efficiency and reduce carbon footprints.

- *Example*: Barcelona uses digital twins to optimize energy distribution across its smart grid network.

4. Public Safety and Security AI-powered digital twins enable real-time monitoring of city infrastructure and activities, enhancing public safety and security. For example:

- *Example*: London has implemented a digital twin to manage and optimize its CCTV surveillance network.

Conclusion

The integration of Physical AI and digital twin technology is driving significant advancements across industries. As these technologies mature, they hold the potential to redefine how we manage and interact with complex systems, offering unparalleled benefits in efficiency, safety, and innovation. However, challenges such as data privacy, scalability, and ethical considerations must be addressed to fully realize their transformative potential.

Chapter 7: Recent Breakthroughs: Intelligent Acting Digital Twins (IADT)

The concept of digital twins has evolved significantly since its inception, transitioning from passive observers to active participants in real-world systems. The emergence of Intelligent Acting Digital Twins (IADT) marks a groundbreaking leap in this technology. Unlike traditional digital twins, which primarily monitor and simulate, IADTs possess the ability to autonomously control and adapt their physical counterparts in real time. This chapter delves into the recent breakthroughs in IADT, exploring their development, applications, and transformative potential across various industries.

1. The Evolution of Digital Twin Technology

- **Definition and Early Applications**: Digital twins were initially developed as virtual replicas of physical systems, used for monitoring and predictive analytics.

- **Transition to Intelligence**: The integration of artificial intelligence (AI) has enabled digital twins to process complex data and make informed decisions.

- **Introduction of IADT**: Intelligent Acting Digital Twins represent the next stage, characterized by autonomy, adaptability, and real-time interaction with physical systems.

2. Key Features of IADT

- **Autonomous Decision-Making**: IADTs can analyze data, predict outcomes, and make decisions without human intervention.

- **Real-Time Adaptation**: These digital twins can adjust their behavior based on changing conditions in the physical environment.

- **Bidirectional Communication**: IADTs maintain seamless communication between the virtual and physical realms, ensuring synchronization and efficiency.

3. Recent Breakthroughs in IADT

- **Development of Adaptive Models**: Researchers have created AI-powered digital twins capable of controlling and adapting their physical counterparts in real time.

- **Applications in Autonomous Systems**: IADTs are being used to control drones, self-driving cars, and robotic systems, enhancing their performance and reliability.
- **Integration with Emerging Technologies**: The combination of IADT with technologies like the Internet of Things (IoT) and 5G networks has expanded their capabilities.

4. Applications of IADT Across Industries

Healthcare

- **Surgical Assistance**: IADTs enable precise control of robotic surgical tools, improving outcomes and reducing risks.
- **Patient Monitoring**: Intelligent twins analyze real-time data from wearable devices to provide personalized healthcare solutions.

Manufacturing

- **Process Automation**: IADTs optimize production lines by autonomously adjusting machinery settings based on real-time data.
- **Predictive Maintenance**: These twins predict equipment failures and initiate maintenance procedures, minimizing downtime.

Smart Cities

- **Traffic Management**: IADTs control traffic systems to reduce congestion and improve safety.
- **Disaster Response**: Intelligent twins simulate emergency scenarios and coordinate real-time responses.

Defense and Aerospace

- **Autonomous Vehicles**: IADTs enhance the performance of unmanned aerial and ground vehicles in complex environments.
- **Mission Planning**: These twins simulate and execute military operations with high precision.

5. Challenges and Ethical Considerations

- **Data Privacy and Security**: Ensuring the confidentiality and integrity of data used by IADTs is critical.
- **Ethical Implications**: The autonomy of IADTs raises questions about accountability and decision-making in critical scenarios.
- **Technical Limitations**: Developing robust and scalable IADT systems remains a significant challenge.

6. Future Prospects of IADT

- **Integration with Quantum Computing**: The use of quantum computing could further enhance the capabilities of IADTs.
- **Expansion into New Domains**: Potential applications in agriculture, education, and entertainment.

- **Vision for the Future**: A world where IADTs seamlessly integrate with human activities, driving innovation and efficiency.

Conclusion

The advent of Intelligent Acting Digital Twins represents a paradigm shift in digital twin technology. By bridging the gap between the virtual and physical worlds, IADTs have the potential to revolutionize industries and improve quality of life. However, addressing the associated challenges and ethical considerations will be crucial to unlocking their full potential.

Chapter 8: Case Studies - AI Factories Leveraging Digital Twins for Power Optimization

The integration of artificial intelligence and digital twins into industrial operations marks a profound evolution in manufacturing and power optimization. In an age of growing environmental awareness and escalating energy demands, industries are pushed to adopt smarter, more sustainable practices. This chapter focuses on how AI factories—complex ecosystems of autonomous systems driven by artificial intelligence—utilize digital twins to revolutionize power consumption, reduce waste, and achieve optimal efficiency. Through the lens of real-world case studies, we will explore the transformative impact of this technology and its implications for the future of energy management.

Understanding Digital Twins and Power Optimization

What Are Digital Twins?

A digital twin is a virtual replica of a physical system, process, or product, continuously updated with real-time data. These dynamic models allow organizations to simulate, analyze, and optimize their operations before making any changes in the real world. By leveraging IoT sensors, cloud computing, and AI algorithms, digital twins serve as powerful tools for monitoring and improving performance across various domains, including power optimization.

The Role of AI in Power Optimization

Artificial intelligence enhances digital twins by enabling predictive and prescriptive analytics. AI algorithms analyze vast amounts of operational data to identify inefficiencies, predict energy consumption patterns, and recommend actionable solutions. For example, AI can determine the optimal time to run energy-intensive machinery based on demand and cost fluctuations.

Why Power Optimization Matters

Power optimization is critical for reducing energy waste, minimizing costs, and achieving sustainability goals. With industries accounting for nearly 40% of global energy consumption, the need for efficient energy management has never been more pressing. Digital twins, empowered by AI, provide a scalable solution to address these challenges.

Case Study 1 – Tesla's Gigafactories

Background

Tesla, a leader in electric vehicle production, has set a benchmark for sustainable manufacturing with its Gigafactories. These facilities are designed to operate with maximum efficiency while minimizing their environmental footprint.

Implementation

Tesla employs digital twins to simulate and optimize its production lines. For instance, the digital twin of a battery assembly line continuously analyzes energy usage across different stages of production. AI algorithms integrated into the digital twin predict potential energy bottlenecks and suggest corrective actions, such as redistributing energy loads or adjusting production schedules.

Results

This approach has led to significant energy savings and improved production efficiency. Tesla's Gigafactories have achieved a remarkable reduction in energy consumption per unit of production, contributing to the company's broader sustainability objectives.

Key Takeaways

Tesla's success demonstrates the potential of digital twins to scale energy optimization across multiple facilities, paving the way for a more sustainable manufacturing ecosystem.

Case Study 2 – Siemens Smart Manufacturing

Background

As a pioneer in smart manufacturing, Siemens has been at the forefront of integrating digital twins into its industrial processes. Siemens' factories produce a wide range of products, from electrical components to automated machinery, making energy efficiency a top priority.

Implementation

Siemens utilizes digital twins in tandem with AI-driven IoT platforms to monitor and optimize power usage. In one case, the digital twin of an industrial motor was used to predict energy consumption based on operating conditions. AI algorithms identified patterns of energy inefficiency and recommended maintenance schedules to prevent energy losses.

Results

This approach has resulted in a 20% reduction in energy consumption and a significant decrease in unplanned downtime. Siemens' use of digital twins exemplifies how advanced technologies can drive both cost savings and sustainability.

Key Takeaways

The Siemens case underscores the importance of combining AI, IoT, and digital twins to achieve comprehensive energy management solutions.

Case Study 3 – General Electric (GE) Renewable Energy

Background

General Electric's renewable energy division is dedicated to producing wind turbines and other clean energy solutions. To meet the growing demand for renewable energy, GE has adopted digital twins to streamline its manufacturing processes.

Implementation

GE's digital twins model every aspect of wind turbine production, from component assembly to final testing. AI algorithms analyze data from IoT sensors to predict energy usage during each stage of production. For example, the digital twin might simulate the energy impact of using different materials or manufacturing techniques.

Results

By optimizing energy consumption, GE has reduced its carbon footprint and improved the efficiency of its production processes. This not only aligns with the company's sustainability goals but also enhances its competitive edge in the renewable energy market.

Key Takeaways

GE's experience highlights the potential of digital twins to align manufacturing processes with environmental sustainability objectives.

Challenges and Lessons Learned

Despite their transformative potential, implementing digital twins for power optimization comes with challenges:

- **High Initial Costs**: Developing and deploying digital twins require substantial investment in technology and infrastructure.

- **Technological Complexity**: Integrating AI, IoT, and digital twins into existing operations can be technically challenging.

- **Skilled Workforce**: Managing and analyzing data from digital twins necessitates a workforce skilled in AI and data analytics.

Lessons Learned

The case studies reveal valuable insights for overcoming these challenges. For instance, partnering with technology providers can help mitigate costs, while investing in workforce training can address skill gaps.

Future Trends in AI and Digital Twins for Energy Optimization

Emerging Technologies

The future of AI and digital twins lies in the development of more autonomous systems capable of real-time energy management. Innovations such as reinforcement learning and edge computing will further enhance the capabilities of digital twins.

Sustainability Goals

As industries strive to achieve carbon neutrality, digital twins will play a critical role in optimizing energy usage and reducing emissions. Collaborative efforts between governments, industries, and academia will be essential to advance these technologies.

Global Impact

The widespread adoption of digital twins for power optimization has the potential to significantly reduce global energy consumption, contributing to a more sustainable future.

Conclusion

The integration of AI and digital twins into industrial operations represents a paradigm shift in power optimization. The case studies of Tesla, Siemens, and GE demonstrate the transformative potential of these technologies to drive efficiency, sustainability, and innovation. As industries continue to embrace these tools, the future of manufacturing looks brighter—and greener—than ever.

Chapter 9: Emerging Trends - Generative Physical AI and Autonomous Digital Twins

The convergence of artificial intelligence, digital twin technology, and advanced analytics is ushering in an era of unprecedented transformation across industries. Among the most groundbreaking advancements in this domain are **Generative Physical AI**, which reimagines the way we design and create physical structures, and **Autonomous Digital Twins**, which autonomously oversee, manage, and optimize physical and digital systems. Together, these technologies embody the next frontier in innovation, enabling organizations to achieve unparalleled levels of efficiency, sustainability, and adaptability.

This chapter will explore the emergence of these technologies, their real-world applications, and the implications they hold for the future. By dissecting key concepts and examining case studies, we will gain insights into how Generative Physical AI and Autonomous Digital Twins are reshaping industries such as manufacturing, energy, healthcare, and urban planning.

Generative Physical AI – Redefining Design and Manufacturing

Pushing Boundaries in Design

Generative Physical AI builds upon the principles of generative algorithms by applying them to physical systems, enabling the creation of designs that would be impossible to conceive using traditional engineering methods. By harnessing machine learning models trained on vast datasets, these systems can explore a multitude of possibilities, optimize designs for specific parameters, and propose novel solutions to complex challenges.

For instance, in the aerospace industry, generative AI has been utilized to design aircraft parts that are lighter yet stronger than their predecessors. These designs often feature organic, lattice-like structures inspired by nature, which balance structural integrity with minimal material usage. This has profound implications for industries seeking to reduce production costs and environmental impact.

Applications in Robotics and Autonomous Systems

Generative Physical AI extends beyond static designs, playing a critical role in robotics. By generating optimized configurations for robotic limbs, sensors, and mechanisms, this technology accelerates innovation in autonomous systems. Robots in manufacturing, healthcare, and agriculture benefit from designs that are not only more efficient but also adaptable to diverse operating environments.

Impact on Manufacturing Efficiency

The integration of generative AI into additive manufacturing (3D printing) has revolutionized how components are produced. AI-driven systems can design components tailored to specific functions, reducing the need for additional assembly and enhancing product performance. For instance:

- **Example:** Automotive manufacturers using generative AI to create optimized brackets that reduce vehicle weight, improving fuel efficiency without compromising safety.

Autonomous Digital Twins – The Rise of Self-Optimizing Systems

Transforming Traditional Digital Twins

While traditional digital twins serve as replicas of physical systems, autonomous digital twins elevate this concept by incorporating self-management capabilities. By leveraging advancements in artificial intelligence, machine learning, and sensor technology, these twins can autonomously monitor operations, predict issues, and execute solutions without requiring constant human intervention.

Applications Across Industries

Autonomous digital twins are revolutionizing several sectors, such as:

- **Smart Cities:** Managing resources, utilities, and infrastructure dynamically based on real-time conditions. For instance, an autonomous digital twin could optimize traffic flow by analyzing congestion patterns and adjusting traffic signals accordingly.

- **Healthcare:** Digital twins of human organs, powered by AI, can simulate patient responses to treatments and autonomously recommend personalized therapies.

- **Energy Management:** Autonomous digital twins in power plants or renewable energy farms monitor energy production, predict maintenance needs, and optimize output to minimize downtime and costs.

Enhanced Adaptability and Predictive Power

Unlike their traditional counterparts, autonomous digital twins adapt to unforeseen changes in their environments. For example:

- A digital twin managing a wind farm may dynamically reallocate energy outputs based on changes in wind patterns and power grid demand, ensuring maximum efficiency.

Synergies Between Generative Physical AI and Autonomous Digital Twins

Bridging the Gap Between Design and Operation

Generative Physical AI and Autonomous Digital Twins complement each other in unique ways:

- Generative AI excels at creating optimized designs for physical systems.

- Autonomous digital twins take these designs into operation, continuously monitoring and improving system performance.

Examples of Synergistic Applications

1. **Smart Factories:** In a factory environment, Generative Physical AI could design an optimized conveyor system, while an autonomous digital twin manages energy use and workflow in real-time to ensure peak efficiency.

2. **Renewable Energy:** Generative AI could design wind turbine blades for maximum aerodynamic efficiency, and autonomous digital twins could oversee their operation, dynamically adjusting output to meet energy demands.

Potential for Fully Autonomous Systems

The convergence of these technologies paves the way for creating entirely autonomous AI-driven systems. For example:

- Autonomous vehicles could benefit from generative AI-designed chassis and engines, combined with digital twins that monitor and optimize their performance during operation.

Challenges and Ethical Considerations

Technical and Financial Barriers

- **High Costs:** The development and deployment of generative AI and autonomous twins require significant investment in hardware, software, and expertise.

- **Integration with Legacy Systems:** Combining advanced technologies with existing infrastructure can be a complex, resource-intensive process.

Ethical Concerns

1. **Accountability:** With autonomous decision-making, ensuring accountability for errors or failures becomes a challenge. For instance, who is responsible if an autonomous digital twin's decision leads to an unintended outcome?

2. **Bias and Fairness:** Generative AI models trained on biased datasets may produce designs that unintentionally perpetuate inequities, such as excluding accessibility features in public infrastructure designs.

3. **Workforce Impact:** The adoption of these technologies could lead to the displacement of jobs, particularly in industries like manufacturing and logistics.

Future Trends and Implications

Advancements on the Horizon

1. **Quantum Computing:** The incorporation of quantum computing is expected to exponentially enhance the capabilities of generative AI, enabling it to explore design possibilities on an unprecedented scale.

2. **Cross-Domain Optimization:** Generative Physical AI and Autonomous Digital Twins may evolve to tackle challenges across multiple domains simultaneously, such as optimizing manufacturing processes while minimizing environmental impact.

Global Collaboration for Sustainable Solutions

These technologies have the potential to address critical global challenges, from climate change to resource scarcity. International collaboration among governments, academia, and industries will be essential to harness their full potential responsibly.

Conclusion

Generative Physical AI and Autonomous Digital Twins represent the next chapter in the evolution of AI technologies, promising to reshape industries and solve complex global challenges. Their convergence signifies a monumental shift in how we approach design, production, and system management. By embracing these innovations responsibly, we have the opportunity to unlock a future defined by efficiency, sustainability, and unparalleled technological advancement.

Chapter 10: Potential Impact on Industries Like Logistics, Healthcare, and Defense

The rapid evolution of AI and emerging technologies has triggered unprecedented changes across industries. Technologies such as digital twins, generative AI, autonomous systems, and machine learning are reshaping traditional operations, creating new opportunities, and addressing long-standing challenges. In this chapter, we'll explore the specific impacts these technologies are having on logistics, healthcare, and defense—three key sectors critical to economic stability, human well-being, and national security.

Each of these industries faces unique challenges, from the need for operational efficiency in logistics, to personalized and accessible care in healthcare, to heightened complexity in modern defense systems. By examining real-world case studies and future trends, this chapter highlights how technological advancements hold transformative potential.

Logistics – Streamlining the Global Supply Chain

Challenges in the Logistics Sector

Logistics forms the backbone of the global economy, ensuring the efficient movement of goods and resources. However, the industry has long struggled with issues such as inefficiencies in supply chains, lack of real-time visibility, escalating costs, and environmental concerns. The rise of e-commerce and global trade has also introduced new complexities that traditional logistics solutions struggle to address.

AI-Driven Optimizations

AI technologies, combined with digital twins and autonomous systems, are revolutionizing the logistics sector by optimizing operations in several key areas:

1. **Real-Time Route Optimization**

   o AI algorithms process live data—such as traffic conditions, weather patterns, and vehicle locations—to dynamically adjust delivery routes, reducing delays and fuel consumption.

   o **Example:** Companies like UPS and DHL use AI-driven systems to optimize delivery routes, saving millions annually on fuel costs while improving service reliability.

2. **Warehouse Automation**

   o Robotics powered by AI are increasingly used in warehouses for tasks like picking, packing, and sorting. Digital twins model warehouse layouts and predict bottlenecks, allowing operators to streamline workflows.

   o **Case Study:** Amazon's fulfillment centers employ AI-powered robots to reduce shipping times and improve inventory accuracy.

3. **Predictive Analytics for Supply Chain Management**

   o Machine learning models analyze historical and real-time data to anticipate demand fluctuations, enabling better inventory management and reducing waste.

   o **Impact:** Enhanced resilience during disruptions, such as global pandemics or natural disasters.

The Role of Autonomous Vehicles

Self-driving trucks and drones are poised to revolutionize transportation and last-mile delivery:

- **Example:** Companies like Waymo and Tesla are piloting autonomous trucks for long-haul freight, reducing reliance on human drivers and cutting operational costs.

- **Challenges and Considerations:** Regulatory hurdles, safety concerns, and public acceptance remain barriers to widespread adoption.

Sustainability and Green Logistics

Digital twins enable companies to model energy usage and emissions in logistics operations, identifying opportunities to reduce carbon footprints. AI can recommend eco-friendly shipping routes and packaging solutions, contributing to greener supply chains.

Healthcare – Revolutionizing Patient Care and Outcomes

Transforming Diagnostics and Treatment

AI technologies are enabling more accurate and timely diagnoses, reducing diagnostic errors, and paving the way for personalized medicine:

1. **AI-Powered Diagnostics**

- Machine learning algorithms trained on medical imaging data identify conditions such as cancer, cardiovascular diseases, and neurological disorders with remarkable accuracy.
  - **Example:** DeepMind's AI system has been applied to retinal scans, detecting conditions like diabetic retinopathy earlier than human experts.

2. **Personalized Medicine**
   - AI analyzes genetic information and patient histories to recommend tailored treatments, optimizing efficacy and reducing side effects.
   - **Case Study:** IBM Watson Health collaborates with hospitals to provide data-driven treatment recommendations for oncology patients.

Autonomous Systems in Healthcare

1. **Robotic Surgery**
   - Surgical robots equipped with AI assist surgeons by providing enhanced precision, reducing complications, and enabling minimally invasive procedures.
   - **Example:** The da Vinci Surgical System has performed over a million surgeries globally, improving patient recovery times.

2. **Digital Twins for Personalized Care**
   - Digital twins of individual patients simulate treatment responses, allowing doctors to test interventions virtually before applying them in real life.
   - **Impact:** Reduced risk in complex medical procedures and improved outcomes.

AI in Healthcare Operations

AI technologies are also streamlining administrative tasks and optimizing hospital operations:

1. **Predictive Analytics for Resource Allocation**
   - AI models predict patient admission rates and resource needs, helping hospitals manage staff, beds, and equipment more effectively.
   - **Example:** AI systems helped hospitals optimize ICU capacity during the COVID-19 pandemic.

2. **Automation in Drug Development**
   - AI accelerates the discovery of new drugs by analyzing molecular interactions and predicting successful drug candidates.
   - **Impact:** Shortened development timelines and lower R&D costs for pharmaceutical companies.

Ethical and Regulatory Considerations

The integration of AI in healthcare raises important questions about data privacy, algorithmic bias, and the ethical implications of machine-based decision-making. These issues must be addressed to build trust and ensure equitable access to AI-driven healthcare solutions.

Defense – Enhancing National Security

The Role of AI in Modern Defense

The defense industry is increasingly leveraging AI and autonomous systems to address the challenges of modern warfare, such as asymmetrical threats, cybersecurity risks, and the need for rapid decision-making.

AI-Powered Intelligence and Surveillance

AI technologies are being used to analyze vast amounts of data from satellite imagery, drones, and other sensors to enhance situational awareness:

- **Example:** AI algorithms identify potential threats in real-time, such as unusual troop movements or suspicious activity in restricted areas.
- **Impact:** Improved intelligence capabilities and reduced risk of human error.

Autonomous Systems in Military Operations

1. **Unmanned Vehicles and Robotics**

   - Drones and autonomous vehicles perform reconnaissance, logistics support, and combat roles without risking human lives.
   - **Case Study:** The U.S. military employs unmanned aerial vehicles (UAVs) like the MQ-9 Reaper for surveillance and precision strikes.

2. **Swarm Technology**

   - AI enables groups of drones or robots to operate collaboratively, executing complex missions with minimal human intervention.
   - **Potential Use Cases:** Search and rescue operations, disaster response, and coordinated defense scenarios.

Cybersecurity in the Defense Sector

AI is playing a crucial role in detecting and mitigating cyber threats:

- **Example:** Machine learning algorithms monitor network traffic, identifying anomalies that may indicate cyberattacks.
- **Challenge:** The rise of AI-powered cyberattacks necessitates equally advanced defenses.

Ethical and Strategic Implications

The use of AI in defense raises significant ethical and strategic questions, including:

1. **Autonomy in Lethal Systems**

   - Should fully autonomous weapons be permitted? What safeguards are needed to prevent misuse?

2. **Geopolitical Risks**

   - The global arms race in AI technologies could destabilize international security if not properly regulated.

Cross-Industry Impacts and Synergies

Convergence of Technologies

The integration of AI, digital twins, and autonomous systems often leads to cross-industry benefits:

- **Example:** Autonomous logistics systems developed for the defense sector are now being adapted for disaster response and humanitarian aid.

Collaborative Innovation

- Partnerships between governments, academia, and industries can accelerate the development and deployment of these technologies, addressing shared challenges such as climate change and resource scarcity.

Conclusion

The potential impact of advanced technologies like AI, digital twins, and autonomous systems on industries such as logistics, healthcare, and defense is profound. By addressing existing challenges and unlocking new possibilities, these technologies are reshaping the way we live, work, and protect our societies. However, their adoption must be guided by ethical considerations, regulatory frameworks, and collaborative efforts to ensure that their benefits are maximized while minimizing risks.

Chapter 11: Vision for the Future – A Fully Integrated AI-Driven Ecosystem

What is a Fully Integrated AI Ecosystem?

Key Characteristics

- **Interconnectivity:** AI systems collaborating across domains, sharing data, and optimizing resources in real time.

- **Autonomy:** Minimal human intervention due to self-learning, self-optimizing AI technologies.

- **Scalability:** Ability to adapt to diverse applications, from local communities to global networks.

- **Accessibility:** Equal access to AI solutions across socioeconomic groups, enabling widespread benefits.

Building Blocks

1. **Artificial Intelligence Models:** Diverse AI systems specialized in tasks ranging from natural language processing to computer vision and robotics.

2. **Digital Twins:** Virtual replicas of physical systems that interact dynamically with real-world environments.

3. **IoT Networks:** Billions of interconnected devices providing real-time data streams for AI systems.

4. **Cloud and Edge Computing:** Infrastructure for storing, processing, and analyzing vast amounts of data efficiently.

Transforming Industries Through Integration

Industry Synergies

In a fully integrated AI ecosystem, industries collaborate rather than operate in silos:

1. **Smart Cities:**
   - AI-driven ecosystems manage energy, waste, transportation, and public safety.
   - Example: Autonomous vehicles, traffic systems, and energy grids working together to optimize urban living.

2. **Healthcare:**

- AI-driven diagnostics, treatment plans, and patient monitoring integrated across global healthcare networks.
- Example: Digital twins of hospitals collaborate to allocate resources during pandemics.

3. **Logistics and Supply Chains:**
   - Unified AI systems predict demand, manage inventories, and optimize transportation globally.
   - Example: Autonomous ships, trucks, and warehouses synchronizing to reduce costs and emissions.

4. **Energy:**
   - AI ecosystems balance renewable and conventional energy sources to meet dynamic demands.
   - Example: Smart grids predicting energy usage and optimizing renewable energy storage.

Societal Benefits of Integration

Economic Growth and Efficiency

- Enhanced productivity across industries due to automated workflows and optimized resources.
- Growth of AI-driven businesses and job opportunities in emerging fields.

Sustainability

- AI ecosystems reducing environmental impact by optimizing energy, transportation, and waste management systems.
- Applications in climate modeling and mitigation strategies.

Global Collaboration

- Unified AI systems fostering international collaboration to address challenges like pandemics, natural disasters, and food security.
- Real-time communication and data sharing between countries.

Enhanced Quality of Life

- Personalized healthcare, education, and public services tailored to individual needs.
- Reduced inequality through access to AI-driven opportunities and resources.

Challenges and Ethical Considerations

Technical Challenges

- Integrating diverse AI systems with varying capabilities, languages, and protocols.
- Ensuring robust cybersecurity to protect interconnected systems.

Social Implications

- Addressing concerns about job displacement due to automation.
- Ensuring AI ecosystems do not exacerbate existing inequalities.

Ethical Concerns

- Protecting data privacy and ensuring transparency in AI decision-making.
- Preventing misuse of AI for malicious purposes, such as surveillance or weaponization.

A Vision for Global Impact

Education and Workforce Development

- Preparing the next generation for AI-integrated careers through education and training.
- AI ecosystems offering continuous learning opportunities tailored to individual skill levels.

Healthcare Transformation

- AI ecosystems eradicating healthcare disparities by providing global access to diagnostics and treatment.
- Predictive models preventing pandemics and improving public health outcomes.

Climate Change and Sustainability

- Fully integrated AI ecosystems addressing climate change through optimized resource management, renewable energy use, and environmental monitoring.

Economic Equality

- Creating equal opportunities for marginalized communities through AI-driven micro-economies and remote work solutions.

Steps Toward Realization

Technological Innovations

- Development of unified AI platforms and protocols for seamless interoperability.
- Investment in cloud and edge computing to support real-time processing.

Policy and Regulation

- Establishing international standards for AI ethics, governance, and security.
- Encouraging public-private partnerships to accelerate adoption.

Public Awareness and Trust

- Educating the public about the benefits and risks of AI-driven ecosystems.
- Transparent communication to build trust in AI technologies.

Conclusion

A fully integrated AI-driven ecosystem represents a bold vision for the future, offering solutions to some of humanity's most pressing challenges. By leveraging the synergy of interconnected technologies, we can create a world that is more efficient, sustainable, and equitable. However, realizing this vision will require collaboration across industries, governments, and communities, guided by a commitment to ethical principles and inclusive progress.

Chapter 12: Final Thoughts on the Transformative Potential of This Nexus:

Revisiting the Transformative Potential Across Industries

The introduction of this nexus—a cohesive, AI-integrated ecosystem—has reshaped how industries function, collaborate, and innovate. Let us delve deeper into the most profound transformations across key sectors.

Manufacturing

The manufacturing industry has transitioned into a realm of mass customization, efficiency, and sustainability. With digital twins and AI working in tandem, factories are now "living entities" capable of optimizing production lines in real time. For instance:

- **Case Study:** General Motors (GM) implemented AI-driven digital twins to replicate entire assembly lines, resulting in significant reductions in waste and production errors. These twins provided insights into energy consumption, pinpointing areas to implement renewable energy solutions.

Looking ahead, this sector is poised to embrace autonomous supply chains, where raw material sourcing, production, and delivery are seamlessly integrated through AI intelligence.

Healthcare

Healthcare stands at the forefront of this revolution, shifting the paradigm from reactive to predictive medicine. The advent of AI-powered digital twins of individual patients promises unprecedented personalization:

- Patients can receive "digital consultations" where their digital twin simulates responses to proposed treatments, optimizing outcomes while reducing risk.

Moreover, AI-driven drug discovery has become exponentially faster. A process that once took years can now happen in months:

- **Example:** AI models recently analyzed billions of molecular compounds to develop antiviral therapies during global pandemics, saving countless lives.

Energy and Sustainability

Energy grids and renewable energy systems now operate in a state of symbiotic intelligence. AI ecosystems ensure dynamic energy balancing:

- Example: Solar farms equipped with digital twins predict weather patterns and adjust energy output distribution accordingly, preventing waste.

This evolution is vital for addressing urgent global challenges such as climate change and resource depletion.

Societal Impacts of the Nexus

The societal reverberations of this nexus extend well beyond industries, permeating everyday life and fostering global interconnectedness.

Human-Centered Innovation

The AI-driven ecosystem has inspired innovations that place humanity at its core:

1. **Smart Cities:** Integrating AI into urban planning allows for more livable and sustainable spaces. Traffic congestion, energy use, and waste management are optimized in real time, enhancing residents' quality of life.

2. **Education:** AI-powered platforms provide personalized learning paths for students, catering to their unique strengths and challenges. These systems can identify gaps in knowledge and adapt curriculums accordingly, ensuring no child is left behind.

Global Collaboration

One of the most remarkable societal impacts is the promotion of collaboration across borders. AI ecosystems facilitate real-time communication and resource sharing, enabling nations to address crises together:

- For instance, during natural disasters, AI systems can predict the impact, coordinate evacuations, and allocate relief supplies efficiently on a global scale.

Work and Productivity

Automation is reshaping the workplace, but it also creates opportunities:

- While some repetitive tasks are replaced, new job roles are emerging in AI supervision, ethical auditing, and system integration.

- AI ecosystems are becoming tools for creativity and innovation, amplifying human potential rather than replacing it.

Challenges and Risks of Integration

As with any transformative leap, this nexus presents challenges that must be addressed with foresight and responsibility.

Technical Hurdles

The integration of diverse systems into a single cohesive ecosystem requires overcoming significant technical challenges:

- **Interoperability:** Ensuring systems developed by different organizations and nations can communicate and collaborate without conflict.

- **Data Overload:** Managing the vast volumes of real-time data generated by interconnected AI systems.

Social Implications

1. **Equity in Access:** Without deliberate policies, the benefits of AI ecosystems could disproportionately favor wealthier nations or communities.

2. **Job Displacement:** While opportunities for upskilling and reskilling exist, proactive measures are needed to prevent social unrest caused by unemployment in certain sectors.

Ethical Considerations

1. **Privacy and Surveillance Risks:** A highly interconnected ecosystem may inadvertently lead to pervasive surveillance and loss of individual privacy.

2. **Algorithmic Bias:** AI systems must be meticulously monitored to prevent reinforcing societal prejudices or inequities.

The solutions to these challenges lie in collaboration and governance, as explored in the next section.

Vision for a Balanced and Equitable Future

The vision of this nexus is not only technological but also deeply humanistic: to create a world where innovation aligns with shared values of equity, sustainability, and collaboration.

Framework for Collaboration

Governments, industries, and academic institutions must form a global alliance to guide the development and deployment of AI ecosystems:

- International standards for ethics, data security, and system interoperability.
- Creation of open-source AI frameworks to prevent monopolies and promote accessibility.

Empowering Underserved Communities

Technologies born from this nexus can be harnessed to uplift marginalized populations:

- Providing remote access to education and healthcare for rural and underserved regions.
- Encouraging entrepreneurship through AI-driven microfinance platforms and localized innovation hubs.

Human-Centric Design

Every aspect of this ecosystem must prioritize enhancing human well-being:

- Smart systems should focus on augmenting human creativity and decision-making, ensuring a complementary rather than competitive dynamic between humans and AI.

Final Reflections

A New Era of Possibilities

The transformative potential of this nexus extends far beyond the domains of AI and technology. It represents a profound shift in how humanity approaches its collective challenges, opportunities, and aspirations. By working together across industries, borders, and disciplines, we can create systems that truly serve the greater good.

A Call to Action

This moment in history calls for leadership, vision, and courage. Stakeholders in every sector must commit to guiding this evolution responsibly:

- Developing policies that protect privacy and uphold fairness.
- Encouraging innovation that prioritizes sustainability and inclusivity.

What's Coming Next

Micro Moves to Macro Wins

I'm writing this book because I believe in the transformative power of small, intentional actions. The concept of "Micro Moves to Macro Wins" resonates with how even the smallest steps, when taken consistently, can lead to extraordinary outcomes. It's about shifting the focus from daunting, large-scale changes to manageable, everyday efforts that build momentum over time.

This book is for anyone who feels overwhelmed by the idea of achieving their goals or creating meaningful change. I want to show that success isn't always about massive leaps; sometimes, it's about those subtle yet powerful movements that accumulate into something life-changing.

By sharing real-life examples, personal stories, and actionable strategies, I hope to inspire others to recognize their own potential for progress—even if it starts with just one small move.

How to connect with me

I value the opportunity to connect with readers, thinkers, and innovators like you! Whether you have questions, feedback, or are simply looking to continue the conversation, here are some ways to get in touch:

- **Email**: Reach out to me at **Contact@FSethi.com** for inquiries, thoughts, or to share your ideas.
- **Social Media**: Follow and engage with me on Linkedin@fsethi or My YouTube channel @fsethi to stay updated with my latest projects and insights.
- **Website**: Visit https://www.fsethi.com for more resources, upcoming events, and exclusive content related to the book.
- **Newsletter**: Follow me on LinkedIn to my blogs for updates on my work, industry trends, and behind-the-scenes stories. You can follow me at https://www.linkedin.com/in/fsethi/recent-activity/articles/
- **Speaking Engagements**: Interested in hosting a discussion or keynote about generative AI and the energy business? Send an inquiry to **Contact@FSethi.com**

I'm always excited to hear from readers—your thoughts, ideas, and perspectives inspire my work. Let's keep the dialogue going!